Healing Journal for Warrior Women

Empower Your Journey with Mindfulness and Reflection

Marika Wessels

Reflections

Description: *Use this space to reflect on your day, your thoughts, and your emotions. Writing down your reflections helps you process your experiences and gain insights into your healing journey.*

Examples:

- "Today, I felt a mix of emotions during my meditation. It was challenging to stay focused, but I felt a sense of calm by the end."
- "I had a difficult conversation with a friend today. Reflecting on it, I realize I need to set clearer boundaries."
- "I noticed that when I practice gratitude, my mood improves significantly. This is something I want to continue doing daily."

In case no one has told you lately, you are incredibly strong and brave for facing your emotions head-on.

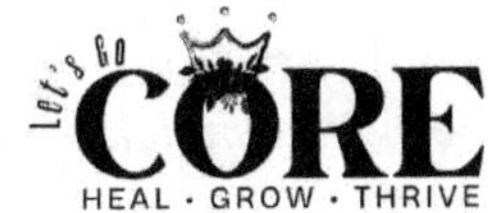

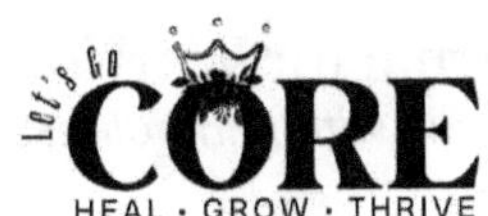

Healing Journal for Warrior Women
Empower Your Journey with Mindfulness and Reflection

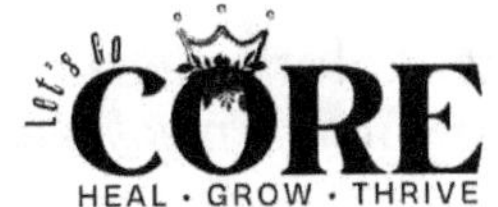

Healing Journal for Warrior Women
Empower Your Journey with Mindfulness and Reflection

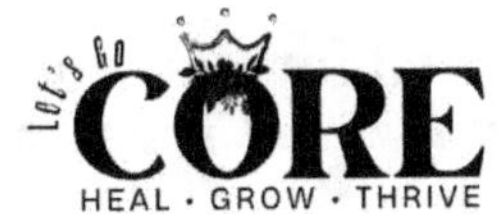

Healing Journal for Warrior Women
Empower Your Journey with Mindfulness and Reflection

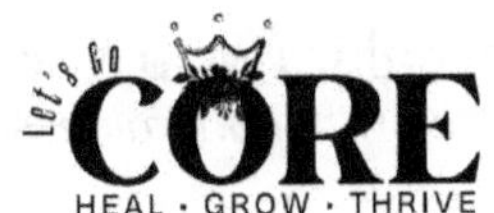

Healing Journal for Warrior Women
Empower Your Journey with Mindfulness and Reflection

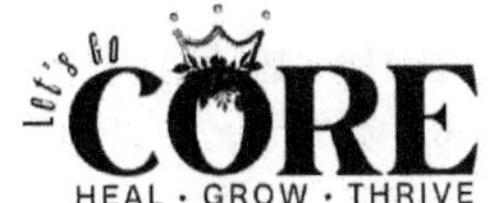

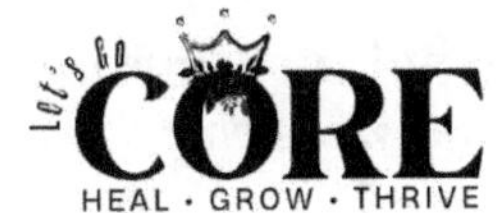

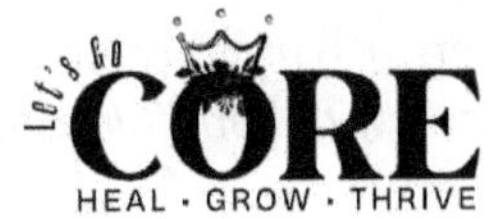

Healing Journal for Warrior Women
Empower Your Journey with Mindfulness and Reflection

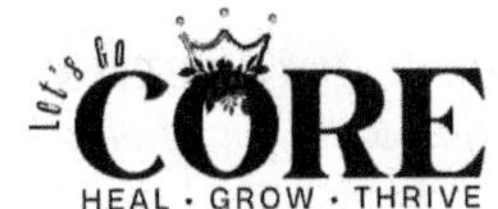

Healing Journal for Warrior Women
Empower Your Journey with Mindfulness and Reflection

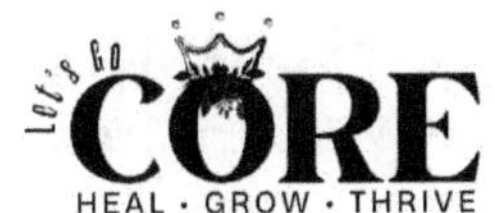

Healing Journal for Warrior Women
Empower Your Journey with Mindfulness and Reflection

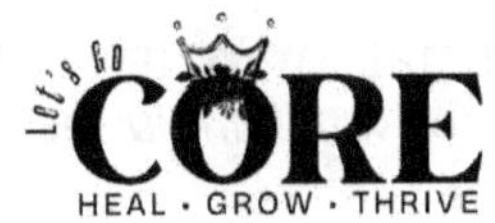

Healing Journal for Warrior Women
Empower Your Journey with Mindfulness and Reflection

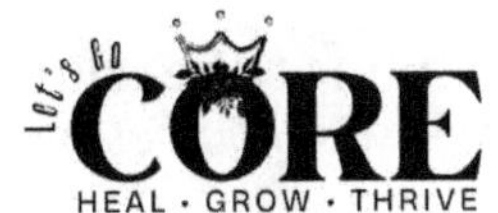

Notes

Description: *Jot down important thoughts, ideas, or reminders. This section is perfect for capturing moments of inspiration, key points from your readings, or any other information you want to remember.*

Examples:
- "Remember to research more about EFT tapping techniques."
- "Idea for next week's journaling prompt: 'What does self-love look like for me?'"
- "Key takeaway from today's reading: Healing is not linear; it's okay to have ups and downs."

In case no one has told you lately, your ideas and thoughts are valuable and worth sharing.

Healing Journal for Warrior Women
Empower Your Journey with Mindfulness and Reflection

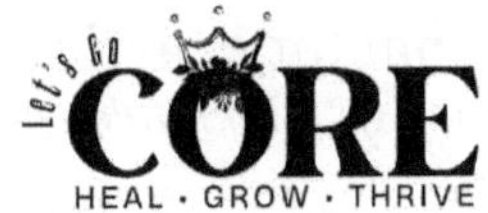

Healing Journal for Warrior Women
Empower Your Journey with Mindfulness and Reflection

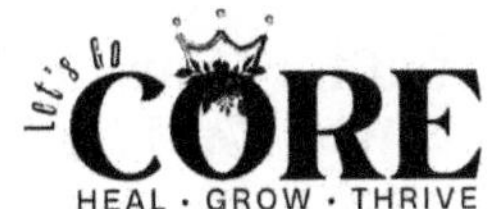

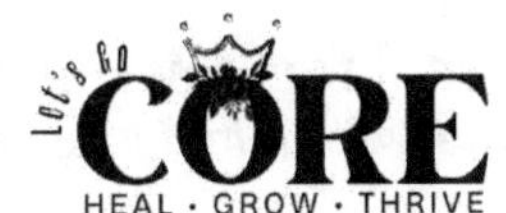

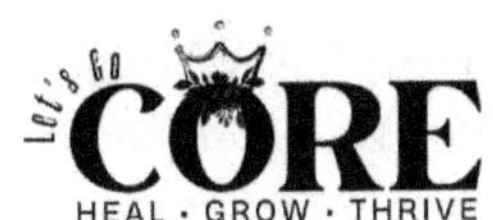

Healing Journal for Warrior Women
Empower Your Journey with Mindfulness and Reflection

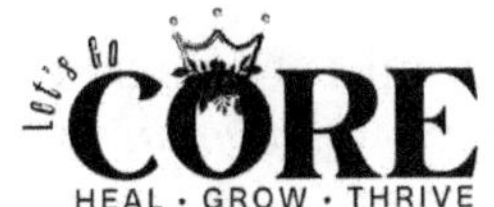

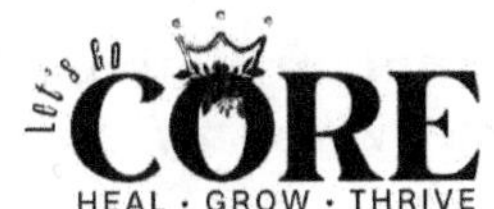

Healing Journal for Warrior Women
Empower Your Journey with Mindfulness and Reflection

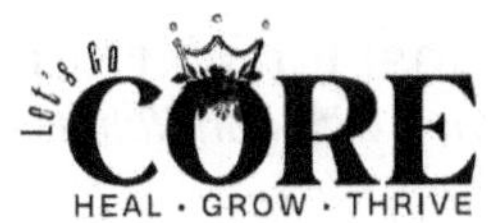

Let's Go
CORE
HEAL · GROW · THRIVE

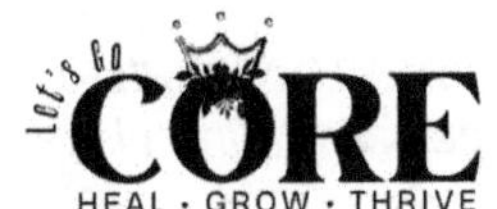

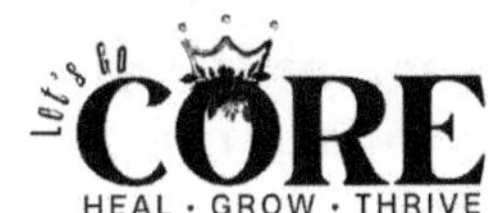

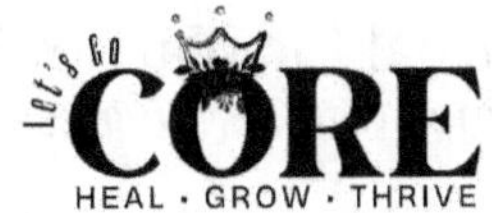

Healing Journal for Warrior Women
Empower Your Journey with Mindfulness and Reflection

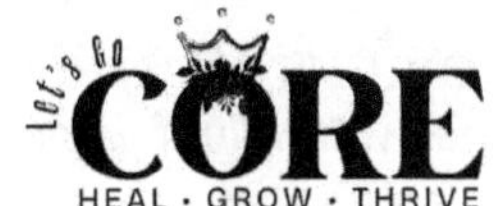

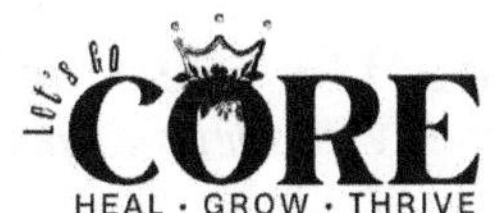

Healing Journal for Warrior Women
Empower Your Journey with Mindfulness and Reflection

Intentions

Description: *Set your daily or weekly intentions here. Writing your intentions helps you stay focused and aligned with your goals. It's a powerful way to manifest your desires and stay committed to your personal growth.*

Examples:
- "Today, I intend to practice self-compassion and speak kindly to myself."
- "This week, my intention is to spend 10 minutes each day on mindfulness meditation."
- "I intend to reach out to a supportive friend and share a part of my healing journey with them."

In case no one has told you lately, your intentions matter and they are leading you towards a brighter future.

Healing Journal for Warrior Women
Empower Your Journey with Mindfulness and Reflection

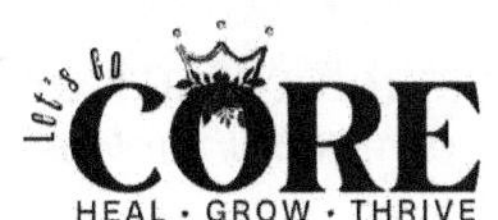

Healing Journal for Warrior Women
Empower Your Journey with Mindfulness and Reflection

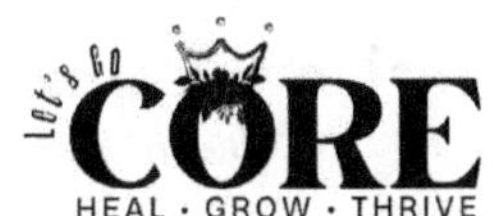

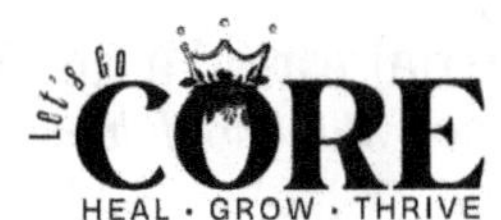

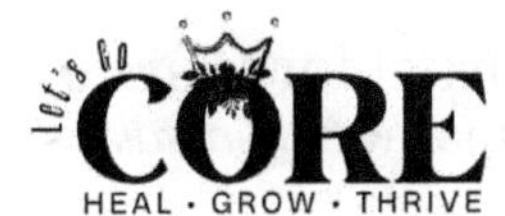

Healing Journal for Warrior Women
Empower Your Journey with Mindfulness and Reflection

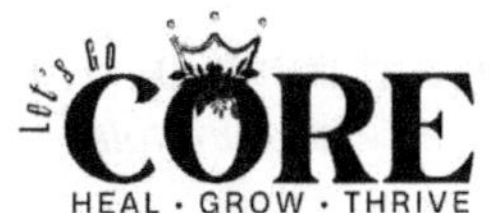

Healing Journal for Warrior Women
Empower Your Journey with Mindfulness and Reflection

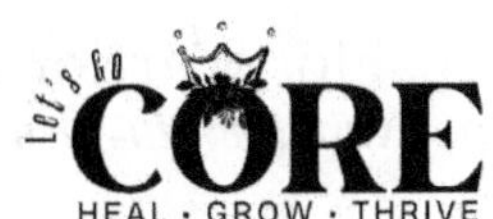

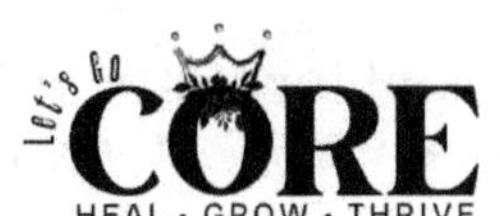

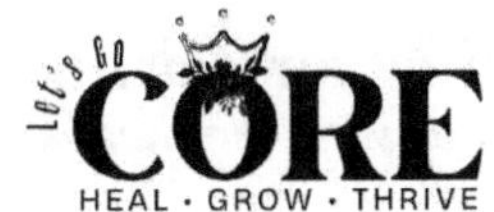

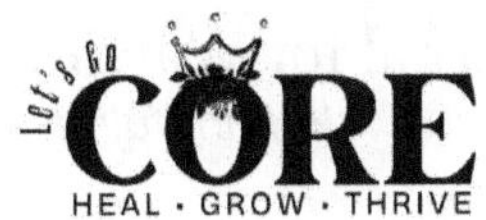

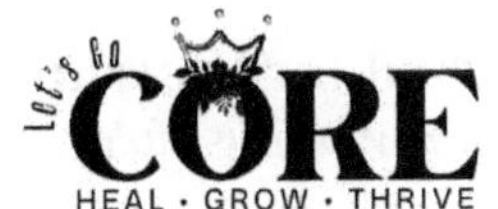

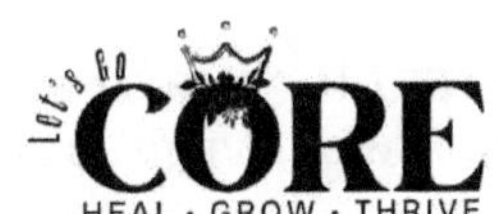

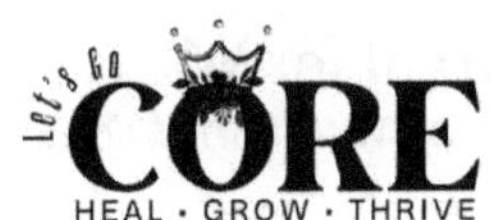

Gratitude

Description: *Take a moment to write down what you are grateful for. Practicing gratitude shifts your focus to the positive aspects of your life and helps cultivate a mindset of abundance and joy.*

Examples:

- "I am grateful for the warm sunshine that brightened my day."
- "I am thankful for the supportive conversation I had with my mentor today."
- "I appreciate having a safe space to express my thoughts and emotions in this journal."

In case no one has told you lately, your gratitude and positive outlook are making the world a better place.

Healing Journal for Warrior Women
Empower Your Journey with Mindfulness and Reflection

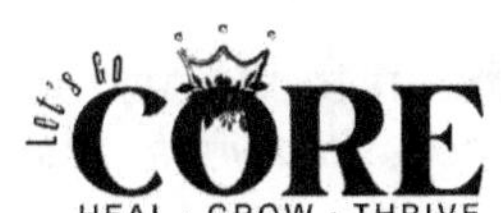
Let's Go
CORE
HEAL · GROW · THRIVE

Healing Journal for Warrior Women
Empower Your Journey with Mindfulness and Reflection

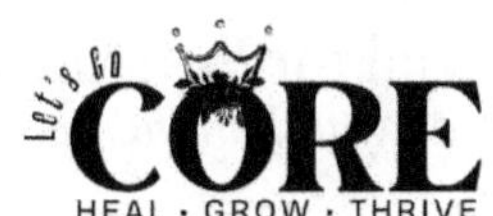

Healing Journal for Warrior Women
Empower Your Journey with Mindfulness and Reflection

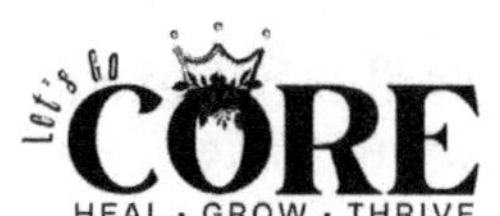

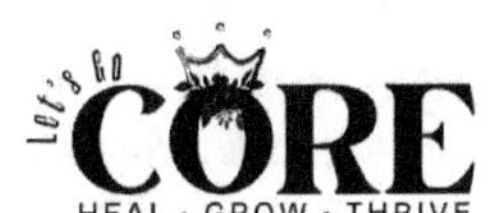
Let's Go
CORE
HEAL · GROW · THRIVE

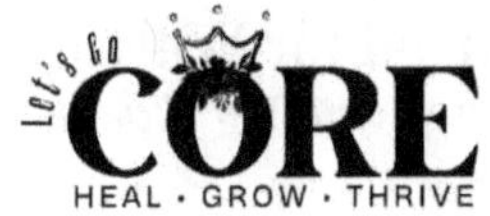

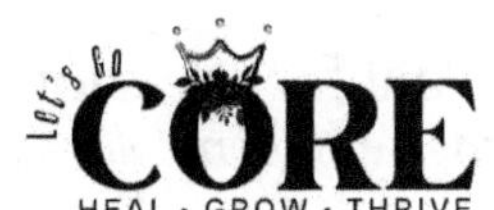

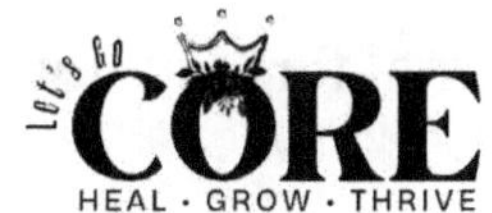

Healing Journal for Warrior Women
Empower Your Journey with Mindfulness and Reflection

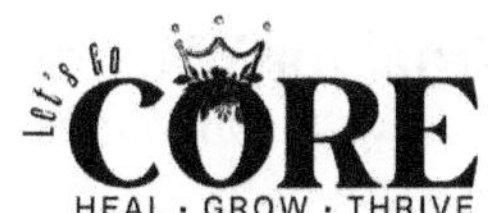

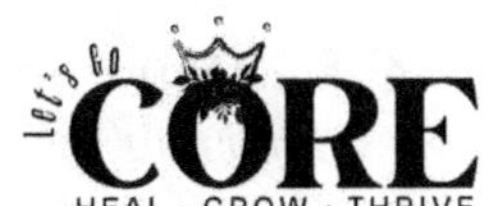

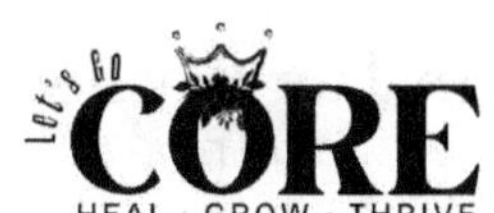

Healing Journal for Warrior Women
Empower Your Journey with Mindfulness and Reflection

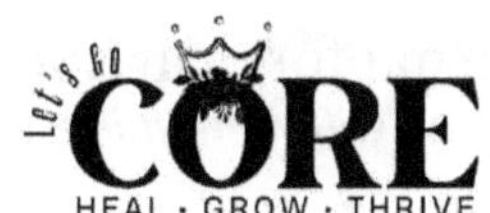

Healing Journal for Warrior Women
Empower Your Journey with Mindfulness and Reflection

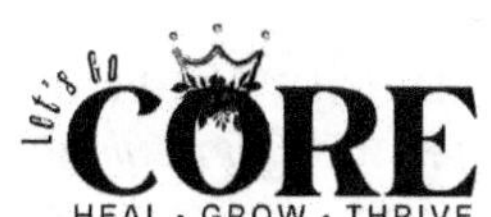